Aberdeenshire Library and Information Service
www.aberdeenshire.gov.uk/libraries
Renewals Hotline 01224 661511

Gowar, Mick, 19

Old Mother
Hubbard ; : Old
Father Hubbard
            JS   Hubbard

2631358

Notes for adults

TADPOLES NURSERY RHYMES are structured to provide support for newly independent readers. The books may also be used by adults for sharing with young children.

The language of nursery rhymes is often already familiar to an emergent reader, so the opportunity to see these rhymes in print gives a highly supportive early reading experience. The alternative rhymes extend this reading experience further, and encourage children to play with language and try out their own rhymes.

If you are reading this book with a child, here are a few suggestions:

1. Make reading fun! Choose a time to read when you and the child are relaxed and have time to share the story.

2. Recite the nursery rhyme together before you start reading. What might the alternative rhyme be about? Why might the child like it?

3. Encourage the child to reread the rhyme, and to retell it in their own words, using the illustrations to remind them what has happened.

4. Point out together the rhyming words when the whole rhymes are repeated on pages 12 and 22 (developing phonological awareness will help with decoding language) and encourage the child to make up their own alternative rhymes.

5. Give praise! Remember that small mistakes need not always be corrected.

First published in 2008 by
Franklin Watts
338 Euston Road
London NW1 3BH

Franklin Watts Australia
Level 17/207 Kent Street
Sydney NSW 2000

Text (Old Father Hubbard)
© Mick Gowar 2008
Illustration © Kate Edmunds 2008

ISBN 978 0 7496 8019 0 (hbk)
ISBN 978 0 7496 8026 8 (pbk)

Series Editor: Jackie Hamley
Series Advisor: Dr Hilary Minns
Series Designer: Peter Scoulding

Printed in China

Franklin Watts is a division of
Hachette Children's Books
an Hachette Livre UK company.
www.hachettelivre.co.uk

Old Mother Hubbard

Retold by Mick Gowar
Illustrated by Kate Edmunds

FRANKLIN WATTS
LONDON • SYDNEY

Kate Edmunds

"My favourite nursery rhyme is 'Sing a song of sixpence'. I have two orange cats called Parsley and Custard. I love to draw them sunbathing in the garden."

Old Mother Hubbard
went to the cupboard,

To fetch her poor dog
a bone.

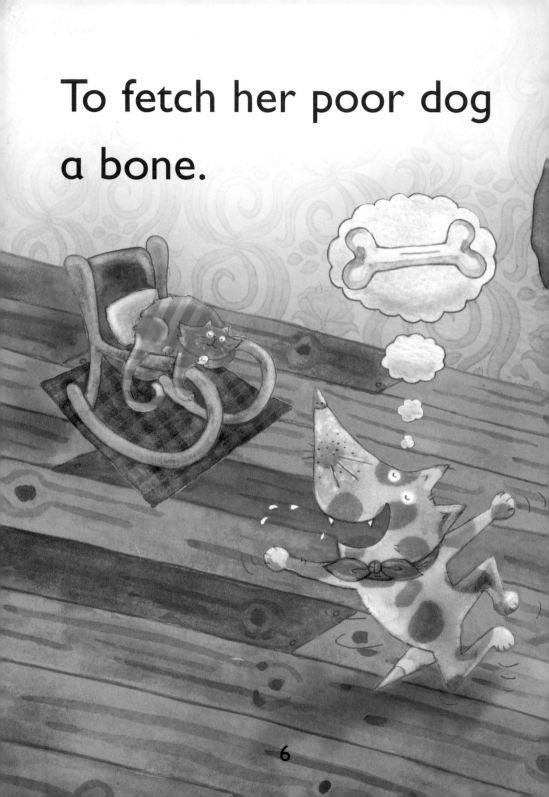

But when she got there
the cupboard was bare.

And so the poor dog had none!

Old Mother Hubbard

Old Mother Hubbard
went to the cupboard,
To fetch her poor dog a bone.

But when she got there
the cupboard was bare.
And so the poor dog had none!

Can you point to the
rhyming words?

Old Father Hubbard

by Mick Gowar
Illustrated by Kate Edmunds

Mick Gowar

"This is me in my shed. This is where I write my books. When I'm not writing I like visiting schools to read my books and tell stories to the children."

Old Father Hubbard
went to the cupboard,

To fetch his poor cat
some fish.

But when he got there
the cupboard was bare.

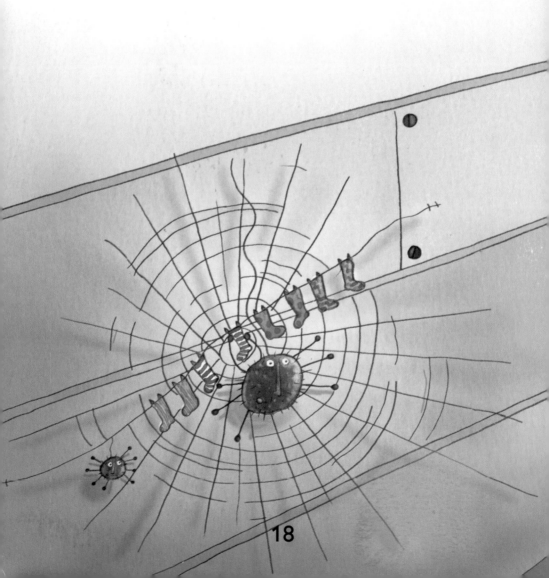

So poor puss got
an empty dish!

Old Father Hubbard

Old Father Hubbard
went to the cupboard,
To fetch his poor cat some fish.

But when he got there
the cupboard was bare.
So poor puss got an empty dish!

Can you point to
the rhyming words?

Answers

There are **11** bones and **5** fish hidden in the picture!

Puzzle Time!

How many bones and fish can you count in this picture?